MW00639496

ISBN 978-0-9914952-0-7
Printed in the USA

For more information visit:
WorryWoos.com

HELPING YOUNG WORRIERS BEAT THE WORRYBUG

A PRACTICAL AND FUN-FILLED GUIDE OF THERAPEUTIC IDEAS AND ACTIVITIES

By Dr. John Irvine • Illustrated by Andi Green

Foundation booklet for The WorryWoo Monster series and companion manual to Don't Feed the WorryBug by Andi Green

Table of Contents:

Isn't it incredible, that in a world where we have more money, more cures, more surveillance and more safety nets... we also have more anxiety than ever before? And our kids are feeling it!

Anxiety is corrosive; it eats away at health and happiness big time. So, if we are going to help our kids through their little worries, we need to understand what worry is all about. After learning some basics regarding how the brain operates, the following activities will make sense and be easier to adapt to your child. These games were developed from an experienced-based combination of many theoretical approaches that have been turned into simple, fun-filled exercises. The result of this research, however, is more important on a deeper level since it allows kids to enjoy life and beat their problems by releasing endorphins into their little systems which, in turn, help fight depression and the feeling that they can't cope.

Before we begin, let me stress that there is no specific way to use this manual. For some readers the games are of primary importance. Others may prefer to begin with the background info. Of course a combination of both would be most effective.

Recommended tools for the following activities include a Wince WorryWoo plush, the WorryBug plush or any other small toy and the book, *Don't Feed the WorryBug.* Although these are fun additions, they are not essential for applying the given techniques.

Wince battles anxiety.

Wince isn't the only one who has to battle the WorryBug—we all do. But some kids can become overwhelmed by their anxieties. While worry is a safeguard that helps us survive, for some kids and adults, it becomes a mind "bug" that destroys happiness and health. The symptom checklist that follows will help caregivers determine whether their child is experiencing normal, helpful worry or whether we're dealing with full-blown anxiety.

What are the Symptoms of Unhealthy Anxiety?

Review the following chart and then rate your child's anxiety level. You may want to use a number system ranging from 1-10. The most frequent/serious characteristics would be rated higher, whereas rare/mild symptoms would be rated lower. For instance, you might rate dry mouth and swallowing difficulties or hoarseness just a 0, 1 or 2 if it's rare in your worrier's symptoms. But, on the other hand, you might rate constant seeking of attention and reassurance maybe 8 or 9 if it's a common characteristic. After you have completed some of the related activities, repeat the process to see how your child is progressing.

Anxiety Symptom Checklist

Symptom	Rating
Dry mouth and swallowing difficulty or hoarseness	☐
Rapid breathing and heartbeat	☐
Twitching or trembling	☐
Muscle tension and headache	☐
Appetite changes	☐
Sweating	☐
Nausea, diarrhea and weight loss	☐
Sleeplessness	☐
Hyperventilation	☐
Irritability	☐
Fatigue	☐
Nightmares	☐
Frequent urination	☐
Memory problems	☐
Constant seeking of attention and reassurance	☐

Worry Bug Staff

What's bugging my child?

If you recognize your child's behavior in the checklist, let's do a bit of detective work to figure out where it's all coming from.

1. First and foremost, take the child for a medical check-up. There are many medical disorders that have similar symptoms to anxiety, so talk to your doctor to rule out any medical causes. If you get the "all clear", move to other checks.

2. Do a parent self-check. If you're an anxious person, then your worrywart may be copying your coping style.

3. Do a management check. Many panicky kids come from homes where parents reward their child's anxiety by fixing it for them. The result is that kids don't learn how to manage their problems, but rely more and more on a parent sorting it out for them.

4. Do a context check. Try to note where and when these anxieties are at their worst. Could it be in the morning before school or upon arriving home in the afternoon? Maybe it's related to an unfamiliar location or activity?

5. Do a home environment check. Is the pace too fast, is the family too busy, is the morning routine chaotic? Is there too much going on after school? And don't forget to take a look at what the kids are watching on TV and DVDs—some are quite scary.

6. Check for any attachment issues. Does the child feel safe and secure with you? Are you super critical of them or yourself? Can your family fix the problem when things inevitably go wrong?

If the above checklist has not provided insight into what may be troubling your child, then it may be time to catch up with a well-respected local clinical child psychologist. They are the professional "mind sweepers" who can delve into more complex issues.

So, let's take a look at some of the thoughts and feelings that might be underlying a child's anxiety experience.

Brain Stuff

Remember, anxiety is meant to be helpful. We're supposed to be anxious when we stand on top of a cliff or walk toward a potentially dangerous animal. Our bodies are designed to help us when we get anxious, primarily by getting us ready to do something about the threat. The problem is that when we feel a strong threat, we stop being able to think about how best to handle it. Instead, we enter into the fight or flight (or freeze) response. This is our brain gearing us for survival. Unfortunately, in humans, this "fight or flight" response comes into play, not only when our physical safety is threatened, but also when our social or psychological safety is under threat.

It explains why a child rejected by his peers may often react as though he has had a near death experience! Don't belittle their response, because in their mind, it's very real and very threatening. When the pressure created by a child's anxiety shuts down the brain, the prefrontal cortex hands over responsibility to the lower subcortical regions. This cuts out a child's capacity to rationally think through the threat. That explains why, when your kids are anxious, all common sense, reasoning and positive thinking go out the window.

One highly underrated technique to get kids out of an anxious state and get their brains back on the job is proper breathing.

If you can get an anxious child to breathe more slowly by practicing some of the techniques in this booklet, the message sent back to the brain is that the threat has passed. The environment is now safe enough to shut down the fight or flight response. The same effect is achieved when we teach kids how to relax their muscles and reduce muscle tension. This gives the brain the message that the danger has passed and it's safe to "come out" and think their way through the situation.

Arming our Kids with "Thought Beating" and "Mindfulness" Strategies

Thought Beating

The fact is that how we think about our world has a great deal of influence over how we feel about our world. For instance, if we think something is easy, our mind will stay confidently in charge. If we think something is a bit of a challenge, that can motivate our mind to take up the challenge. However, if we think something is a big threat, it becomes "emotivating" and forces us to react "emotionally", rather than rationally. The mind becomes overwhelmed and the brain stem, "the feelings gate," takes over with a fight or flight response. This takeover by the brain stem (amygdala) is sometimes referred to as the "amygdala hi-jack."

Another peculiar part of our thinking which deals with worry refers to the tendency of the self-fulfilling prophecy to come true. That is, the self-imposed notion that something (usually bad) is going to happen, without any basis, just because we say it will. Sometimes our kids fear something and carry out some ritual to avoid it happening; for example, checking all the doors again and again to make sure they're locked. Assuming no burglars have come in that night, their little mind says "Just as well I checked: it stopped anyone from breaking in!" So the next night, using this rationale, they're more likely to use the same technique, making the ritual become compulsive.

Beating worry requires both a physical effort—slower breathing and relaxed muscles—as well as a mental effort to distinguish "worry thoughts" from rational thoughts. But knowing what our "inner self-talk" is saying isn't necessarily that easy, especially for little kids. That's why I've used the WorryBug as the vehicle to help young kids separate good, helpful thoughts from thoughts that make us worry more and "feed the WorryBug". As children get older, they become more aware of and can identify their thoughts. The more they're aware of their thoughts, the greater the chance that they'll be able to keep their minds on top of their worries, especially if they have learned how to control their breathing.

Mindfulness

This may sound like a buzzword, but "mindfulness" has become very important in our therapy options. Unlike thought blocking tactics or talking back to the annoying WorryBug, in this technique we accept a worrying thought but we don't dwell on it or get caught up in the emotions it evokes. In other words, it's as if we're watching our thoughts from above—like they're marshmallows going along a conveyor belt in a production line. Our worrying thought is just one more marshmallow, not bigger or more important than the others. As such, it certainly won't be given permission to be so important that it shuts down the conveyor belt and blocks up the system. You might start with an example so the child understands how it works. For instance "I'm having the thought that I won't be able to cope with school tomorrow." We then teach our children not to judge this thought or put more emphasis on it than another thought, but rather just to observe it. Then, watch the next thought that comes along: perhaps, "now I'm thinking it would be nice to have some dinner." This teaches kids to realize that our brains produce all types of thoughts. Thoughts that once got them "all worked up" can now be "watched and let go" along with the others.

Once children get the hang of how mindfulness works, you can suggest they might want to see what happens in their "personal factory" if you mention a thought. You might mention the words "going to school" or "being in the dark" or whatever their worry is. Let them take in that thought, put it on their conveyor belt, and see what thought comes next. Even if they say that the next thought is something like "I'm scared"—that too, is just another thought which goes on the conveyor belt only to be replaced by another. **Your child will learn that worrisome thoughts really don't have much power if they don't get a reaction.** So the next time the worry thoughts comes up, they'll be more likely to let it go.

By staying calm and observing thoughts, kids begin to realize that the worry that once created serious tension can come and go without becoming a big deal.

Parents also need to be more mindful of their parenting self-talk. They should be aware that thoughts like "I'm not coping" and "I can't deal with this child" are simply "thoughts" —not the truth, not definite guides, not helpful—just thoughts. This means that when these self-defeating thoughts come along, parents, like their kids, should acknowledge them and then allow them to pass without strong emotional reactions. The point is that both adults and children have worries. It is up to us to give our kids the strategies and confidence to handle their anxieties. That's probably one of the best legacies any parent can offer.

The ideas, which I've presented, represent two slightly different ways to help your child deal with anxious thoughts. One approach identifies and directly combats the worrisome thoughts using "thought beating strategies". The other tactic uses "mindfulness strategies", which teach the child to calmly identify the worries and let them pass, rather than dwell on them. Try to find out, which, if not both, is most effective for your child. Finally, just keep in mind that addressing entrenched anxious thinking can be very hard. Remember, if the tools in this book don't make the impact you were hoping for, professional psychological input may be needed.

Building Quality Attachments

The good news is that there is one very powerful force against the tricks that children's minds play on them—their relationship with you! This is called "attachment". The quality of their attachment with the primary caregiver, usually the mother, has a huge bearing on how a child handles his/her world. This applies whether the child feels confident or afraid, competent or incompetent, lovable or unlovable. As for the kids who suffer from anxiety, if they do have high-quality attachment, it acts as a foundation for successful coping. Armed with high-quality attachment, the growing child has the confidence to form good quality attachments with other adults with whom they come in contact. This further enhances the child's sense of self.

The main point is for teachers and other caregivers to recognize the importance of the role they play in a child's life. When a boy or girl comes from a home in which family relationships are dysfunctional and the attachment systems are less than optimal, these other individuals are essential in helping a child feel secure and less threatened.

A secure attachment, not an overprotective one, means that a parent not only understands a child's needs but is also able to respond to those needs.

This especially pertains to their care, comfort, and security. If kids feel secure with us, they're more confident to leave us, explore and grow. Then, if they should ever feel overwhelmed by life, they're more comfortable returning to us as their haven. In the process of repeating this cycle, the fact that they can consistently trust in a caregiver provides the child with a sense of security and confidence to deal with their world and their relationships.

However, life isn't perfect; we're not perfect. We have many pressures on us, and it's not always possible to meet all our kids' needs. Writer Alvin Toffler noted, "Parenting is the last province of the amateur!" This implies that we will all make mistakes. The important thing is to show our kids how to go about repairing a mistake. It is this ability to do good repair work, and not merely the absence of disruptions, that is the hallmark of secure attachment between parent and child.

Repairing relationships is all about stepping back and looking at what we did—or didn't do—in meeting our child's needs. It means addressing an issue calmly and in a kind way with our child. First we may want to talk about what we both did that wasn't helpful. Then we identify how it felt when we both acted in that "unhealthy" way. But most importantly, we must discuss how we will handle a similar problem should it arise again.

The Insecure Child

Of course, some kids are more secure than others. To a certain degree, it has to do with genes, the birth process, early experiences and the myriad of things that make life so complex.

The following list includes some parenting practices that can make kids feel less secure which are within our control to change.

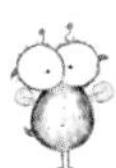

Inconsistency - Inconsistency in our primary caregiving roles regarding routines, discipline and our expectations can create confusion and insecurity for our children.

Perfectionism - If either parent has very high expectations of themselves and their family, it can threaten a child's sense of adequacy. Children can grow up feeling they are only lovable when they get things "right".

Permissiveness - Kids need boundaries! The absence of clear and consistent boundaries means that children are unprotected and feel very vulnerable. When a child fears a parent can't cope with his or her behavior, they also wonder whether a parent can protect them. This can lead to significant insecurity, usually in the form of boundary pushing and defiance, as he/she repeatedly looks for some adult to "take control".

Criticism - Criticism raises a lot of self-doubt and anxiety in our children. Often the critical parent is subconsciously repeating and passing on the criticism they received as kids. If you tend to be critical in your approach to your child, try to balance your feedback by making a rule with yourself that for every negative comment, you will also give two positive ones. Alternately, as soon as you hear yourself going into negative territory, change your thoughts to constructive things you would want your child to do to fix the situation.

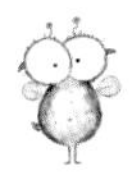

Adult Confidante - Adult worries are not for children. Some parents, maybe because they have no other adult to lean on, prematurely burden young kids' minds and freedom with the worries of an adult world. Little kids can't cope with that. They have no understanding or perspective, so burdening them with grown-up worries is very distressing. It also makes them wonder "who is taking care of whom?" When our kids feel they have to take care of us they will stop sharing their own concerns with us for fear it will make us feel worse. Often this child can look like he's okay but internally feels quite distressed.

Guilt vs. Shame

Guilt is an important and powerful emotion. Its presence is intended to motivate us to change when we've done something wrong. However, problems arise when parents make the mistake of labeling the child as somehow "bad" rather than focusing on the bad behavior. When this happens, we've changed the guilt (which is sometimes helpful) into a sense of shame. Shame is not helpful because it teaches children not to like who they are, instead of disliking what they did.

Parental Modeling

Children are like emotional litmus paper:

they soak up the vibes. If parents are constantly worrying about work, weather, home chores, money, mother-in-law, lack of time or other trials, the child picks up the anxious vibes and also copies the anxious behavior. Conversely, always pretending that everything is fine and that you have no worries doesn't give your child exposure to reality and a model where anxious feelings and thoughts can be addressed and managed.

So don't hesitate to show your kids how you handle your worries. If it's not going to be frightening for the kids, discuss those worries. Do not approach these conversations in a way that suggests you are overwhelmed, but rather identify the source of the worry and how you plan to deal with it. Families can play a game of "highs" and "lows", asking "What was best part of your day? What was the worst? How did you handle the worst? What can we do to help each other through those low points and how do we celebrate our successes?"

How do I get my worrier to tackle the WorryBug?

Wince Worry Winning Strategy

After you have gone over the checklist(p8), there are a variety of activities you can undertake as a parent or caregiver. Since you know your child best, you may want to begin with a general, casual conversation in which you introduce the child to the WorryBug or a similar, small cuddly plush. Hug it, touch it and talk to it. Doesn't it feel nice? Allow the child to become friendly with this new non-threatening friend. Once you have gotten this far, you may want to share the following experiences:

- Together, read the book *Don't Feed the WorryBug.*
- Explain that the WorryBug is just a soft little toy that can't hurt anyone. You may want to emphasize that, "He's nothing but a mischievous imp who's trying to tease Wince."
- Whenever your little worrier is worrying, you may want to start a conversation by sitting the soft toy on one knee and the worrier on the other.
- Ask your child if he remembers the things that Wince worried about in the book: chores, homework, lost possessions, etc.
- Next, turn the attention to your child. See if he/she can identify things that they personally worry about. They may bring up serious issues like something happening to a family member or being alone or rejected by friends. Other worries may be more "kid-centric" such as storms, large animals, spiders, making mistakes… or that dreaded monster in the closet or under the bed.
- Because kids are very suggestible, it would be best NOT to give examples of your own worries, since children may take your worry and make it their own. But if they cannot identify any worries, you can help by identifying some of your own that are outside their range of experiences, such as getting home late from work, keeping the house tidy, etc.
- Finally, talk about the fact that everyone has worries, including adults.
- Together, try to come up with some ideas on how we can all beat the WorryBug. The following games and activities will "jump start" the process!
- After deciding on a "game plan", do some cuddling, storytelling or a relaxation activity.

These activities are not just for clinically anxious kids but for all kids who, like adults, carry a few little worries from time to time but lack the experience or maturity to know how to handle them.

Games and Activities

Now, if you're ready and well-armed, let's get cracking with some activities to help your kids handle their worries!

1. The "What If" Worry Winning Game

This strategy teaches kids to arm themselves with ideas ahead of time, rather than anxiously await the fickle finger of fate.

- Encourage the child to work out, on their own, some ways to handle their fears so that they will become winners. For example, if the fear is mommy being late in picking me up from school, the child would think about what action/s they could take should they be in this position.
- Add a few suggestions, if needed, after they have given you their ideas.
- Have them choose the best approach for their situation. Talking things over with you will help boost the child's self-esteem. Hopefully they've learned that a worry shared is a worry spared.

> "If children can come up with confident solutions to their worst fears or "worst case scenarios" on their own, the fear factor drops enormously."

2. The Worry Winning Ladder

This activity builds self-confidence

- Have children list or tell you all their worries. If the child can count, tell him/her to rate each worry from 1 to 10 (big worries are given high scores and little worries given low scores). Younger kids who aren't sure of their numbers might just tell you whether the worry is big or little.
- Draw a ladder with several rungs and call it the WORRY WINNING LADDER—generally one rung for each worry mentioned plus an extra rung at the bottom for some worry you know they don't have (explained below).
- Place the worry you know they don't have (e.g.: fear of the pet dog) on the bottom rung.
- Put their lowest ranked worry on the next rung up. The other worries will go on higher rungs in ascending order as indicated by their worry rating score. The most important worry will sit on the top rung.
- Ask the child to distinguish between which worry is the worst, should several worries have the same score. When an adult points out to a worried child that they've already beaten the bottom one on the list (the least worrisome) this boosts the child's belief that they can beat others. They become motivated to tackle the more difficult worries. It also helps to develop self-confidence and a "can-do attitude."
- Give them your applause as they conquer the easy ones. This builds up their confidence to beat the next one on the ladder.
- Draw or write an incentive above the top rung as the prize for "beating their worries." This could be a trip to the zoo, a movie, a toy—whatever the parent and child decide.

3. Power Stone Magic

This activity is very effective, especially if you have ever done any magic tricks with the kids. The emphasis in this game is to shift "bad" or negative imagination to "good" imagination.

- Get some colorful polished gems, available at many craft stores, and put them in a special box.
- Bring the stones out when the child is really burdened by some big worry. Then ask your child, with closed eyes, to feel them and choose three that feel very good or soothing.
- Have the child open their eyes, look at their choices and pick the one that feels and looks the best.
- Take the stone they've chosen, put your loving "magic hands" around it and say something like "I've put my magic powers in there so that you can now beat the WorryBug. You don't have to be afraid of him anymore."
- Suggest that the child take that stone and put it on the table near their bed calmly repeating that the very thing they fear won't happen. If it's something that might happen like catching germs, explain that they will have the power to beat it!

"By the way, if the child is afraid of something like catching germs, I excitedly tell them about the army of good soldiers marching up and down in their blood stream ready to fight germs. If they are worried about a bad virus that is making them sick, you can tell them that their soldiers are in the midst of a big battle which they will win! And when they do, they will take the beaten germs captive and make them part of their own army so that they will be stronger than ever."

- If the child needs an additional stone for school, he/she can pick a second favorite stone that can go in their school bag "for protection."

4. Word & Image Lifter Games

The following Word and Image Lifter Games attempt to reach out to two very different styles of worriers. These games try to distinguish kids who use words to get themselves into an anxious state, from those children who use images to visualize something anxiety producing, such as mom at home having a good time with the baby while they're stuck at school.

4A. Word Lifter

This strategy helps to separate silly fears from sensible worries.

- First, make up a list of silly fears like the sky is falling or there's a T-Rex in the garden so kids get the concept of sensible versus silly fears. Next, make a list of other real (even if silly to us) fears they might have such as "Mom might forget to pick me up after school and I might have to sleep there" or "No one wants to play with me". Finally, make a third list of sensible fears like "If I run across the road I might get hurt" and "If after school I don't wait for mom in the spot where she told me to be, she might not be able to find me" etc. Use this latter list to teach good, healthy safety measures.
- See if the kids can separate **silly** fears that the WorryBug loves, from **sensible** fears that they have been warned about.
- Then emphasize that the WorryBug is having fun by making them unhappy. Teach them to say, "Stop, WorryBug, you're just a soft toy with silly ideas, I will not listen to you."
- Reinforce how clever they are if they understand the difference, or help them with ideas if they can't.

4B. Word Lifter

This is another activity that works well with kids who think their way into an anxious state.

- Help the child identify some thought which made them start to worry. (e.g. "I'm a loser" or "no one likes me")
- Have them say to themselves (or the Worry Bug, if you're using an externalizing aid), "Stop! You're making me sad!"
- Then find a good word or mantra that they can put in the place of the rejected bad one (e.g. "Natasha and Louise are my friends and I know that they like me and I like them"). Just help them choose and use words that are true and uplifting so that they don't spiral down the worry road.

4C. Word Lifter

This is similar to a fill-in-the-blank activity. It helps soften worries by having kids express what is bothering them by completing part of a sentence.

"Add a Tail" Game:

If the child knows their typical worry thought (e.g. "I can't leave mom") then get them to add a "tail" or ending based on their actual experience.

For example:
Worry: "I can't leave mom________________"
Tail: "BUT I've done it over 500 times since I was born and I actually can do it!" or "The WorryBug often lies to me so maybe I can leave mom."

"Add a Beginning" Game:

This is like the one above and can be used with it. Instead of starting with "I can't leave mom," they could say, "I'm having a WorryBug thought— that I can't leave mom." They have now identified the fear as being WorryBug induced and it's not really true.

One of the best programs I have ever seen along these lines is the "Get Lost Mr. Scary" program. It's well worth checking out if you deal with kids from five to seven years of age. For additional information go to www.getlostmrscary.com.au. At the bottom of the home page is the link to register and find out details of the program.

5. Image Lifter

This activity is for kids who imagine or visualize their way into an anxious state as opposed to children who talk their way into an anxious state.

- Help the child replace a worrisome image by visualizing a better one. For instance, they may have an upsetting image of kids laughing at them when they have to present a project at school. Instead, set up an image of them being self-assured as they explain their project to a group of really interested students.
- Remember to practice the new image until it is powerful and comfortable.
- When you feel that the new image is securely in place, then recall the nasty old image. The idea is to see if the child is able to readily switch back to the new image with its different and better feelings.

This technique can also be used to remedy bad dreams.

> "In our clinic, I once encountered a little boy named Timmy. He couldn't sleep because he would visualize a bad man coming into the bedroom. Together, we came up with the following solution: I gave Timmy a little piece of stick-um that would act as a button which he would put on the side of his bedside table. We imagined that as the man opened the door, young Timmy would press the sticky button, and the door would slam shut in the intruder's face—no matter how many times he tried to open it! In the meantime the police would be on their way to arrest the bad guy! The next day Timmy's name and photo would be in the papers, and he would be a hero in the eyes of his friends. The good thing about imagination is you can do with it whatever you like, but the good stuff has to outshine the bad if it's going to work. It certainly did for Timmy."

6. Face Lifter

- Draw a circle and divide it into six equal sections. Each section will represent a different mood: happy, sad, grouchy, peaceful, angry and worried. Then hang this "feelings" chart on the wall like a clock.
- If the child comes out of their room with the face that spells trouble for the family (e.g., angry), you can ask him/her what's on their mind. If they refuse to discuss it with you, as a soft form of time-out, you can then send them back to their room for a "Face Lift." First describe the look that is on their face, be it sad, angry or grouchy. This will, in turn, explain why they need a "Face Lift."
- Tell the child that they can come out of their room when they choose to wear a more agreeable face. This is also a good exercise to teach young kids to learn how to read other people's body language and feelings.

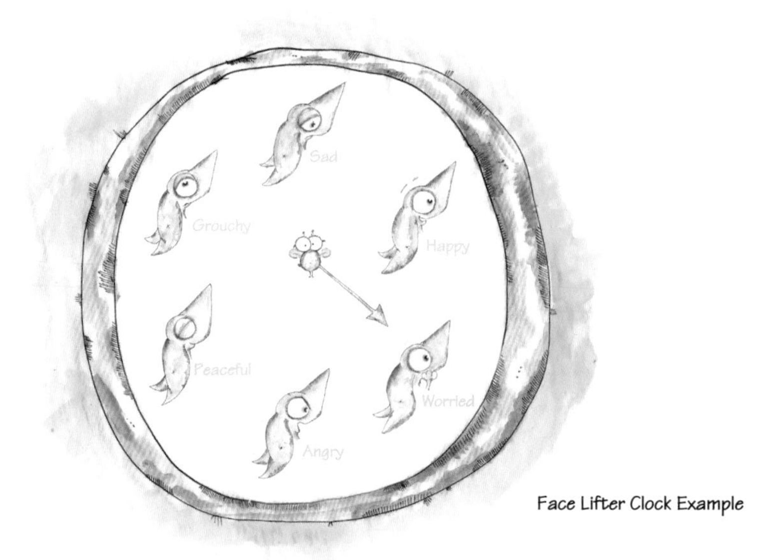

Face Lifter Clock Example

A note to parents: Sometimes kids use "negative attention seeking" or just "acting down" (sad, grouchy, whining, etc.) to get attention. Others may "play up" (clowning, interrupting etc.). The preceding exercise indicates that the adult has given the child the chance to share or explain why they're angry or grouchy. So by suggesting that the child can go back to their room and change their "dial", it encourages children to share and communicate what is going on, if they're genuinely sad or worried, or else change their game if he/she is just attention seeking. Too many parents spend time chasing after kids asking them "what's wrong?" when there's really nothing wrong. Often they're acting down to get as much attention as they can to retain their place as the center of attention. This is not good for the kids, the parents or their relationship.

7. SMILE!

When you look happy, everyone feels better!

Smile. You probably know that if you're down or worried, one technique that works is to just lift the corners of your mouth into a smile. The brain can't tell the difference between a happy smile and a fake smile, so either way you'll start to feel better with a grin.

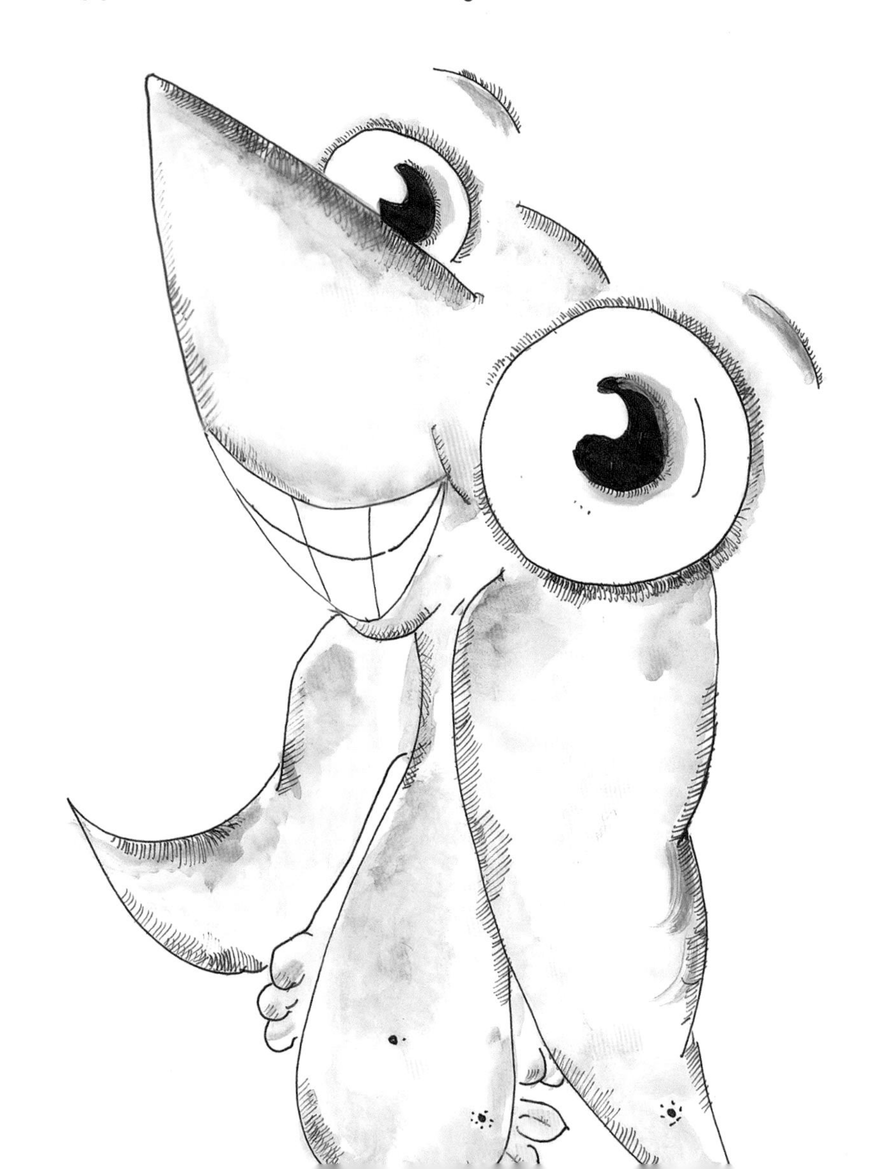

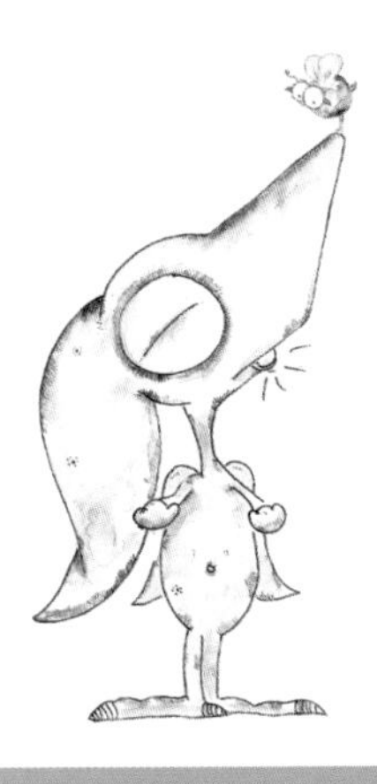

8. Relaxation

The following techniques can be used by the entire family to relax their body and mind. Choose the style that best suits your child's age and personality.

Body Relaxation

- **Hands and arms** - Have the child pretend to be squeezing an orange. When it's all squeezed out they let it drop and let their muscles relax.
- **Arms and shoulders** - Invite the child to pretend that they are a cuddly cat that's stretching. Have them raise their arms high over their head, then back to their side, then out in front, then up to the ceiling, dropping arms down in between.
- **Shoulders** - Let the child pretend that they are a turtle that senses danger. Have them pull their head tight into their shoulders—right up to their ears if they can. When the "danger" has passed, they can relax and come out into the warm sunshine.
- **Jaws** - Have the child imagine that they have a chewy caramel in their mouth. They carefully bite down on it—hard, and then let their jaw relax. Repeat several times.
- **Face and nose** - Suggest to the child that an annoying fly has landed on their nose. They have to get it off by wriggling and wrinkling their nose. Then it flies away but comes back. So, they repeat the wrinkling and wriggling again.
- **Stomach** - Explain to the child that when we worry, the muscles in our tummy become all gnarled and knotted like the roots of a tree. Then, imagine little leaves falling to the bottom of their tummy, one at a time, gently landing. Each leaf unknots the muscles a bit, and then down comes another, etc. Encourage them to notice and enjoy the difference in their tummy tension.
- **Legs and feet** - Ask the child to pretend to push their toes down into soft oozing mud. Have them spread their toes, relax, and then step out of the mud and relax.

Breathing Relaxation

- Use a bubble wand to teach children how to take deep breaths. Have them breathe in slowly and then breathe out into the wand to make the world's BIGGEST bubble.
- Practice breathing into a tissue. Have the child hold it in front of their face. Then have them blow on it until it's horizontal and they can see your face.
- Help kids learn "alternate nostril breathing". Gently rest the index finger and thumb on either side of the nose. Take a breath in; lightly press the left nostril and exhale through the right. Lightly press the right nostril to inhale through the left. Keep repeating this cycle. Alternate nostril breathing is a great way to help settle panicky kids.
- You can assist kids with their slow breathing by helping them to count from one to three. Count with them (1, 2, 3) as they breathe in; do it again as they breathe out. Have them do this for one to two minutes. Next, have them say their troublesome thought slowly, in a relaxed voice (e.g. "I can't talk in front of the class").
- Then, as explained in the Word Lifter game (#5), add top and tail thoughts to the following sentence: "I'm having a WorryBug thought that I can't talk in front of the class, BUT I know I can because I've done it before." This may take a bit of practice, but keep at it. The slow breathing will help to reinforce the child's capacity to be less distressed by the worry.
- With older kids who love the ocean, you can achieve good breathing slowdown by getting them to imagine waves rolling in to shore on the exhale and then breathing in as the wave recedes.
- Choose the breathing activity that best suits the age and interest of the child. The general rule is to practice for one to two minutes or until the child feels they have their breathing back under control.

9. Relaxation Aids

Stress levels can be lowered through the use of the following:

Soft toys - While your child is cuddling up to Wince or another soft toy, introduce the WorryBug. Explain how the cute little plush is just a soft toy—nothing to be frightened of. You may want to add "Remember that the WorryBug gets bigger with every worry that you feed him!" Impress upon the child that the goal is to make sure the WorryBug stays small and cute and doesn't become a needless "monster" that ruins their happiness.

Books - Sharing a reading moment and cuddling around a story book is always relaxing and something children look forward to.

Pets - The role of pets in getting kids to relax is well researched. Choose a cuddly/friendly pet that makes your child feel loved and valued. If you do this, however, make sure the choice is a pet that you also want, because kids' promises to feed and look after pets are rarely matched with action.

Calming corner - Have a "calming corner" somewhere out of the way. It must be quiet with no noise or interruptions. Anyone can go there when they're stressed to listen to soft music, read a book or magazine, do a puzzle or any comforting action, such as brushing one's hair.

Water relaxation - Most kids love water to unwind their little systems. Add soft music and dim lights if needed, so they can soak up the soothing atmosphere. (To ensure a safe bath time, lighting should always be kept at a level where surroundings are fully visible.)

Music relaxation - Make your own musical relaxation collection. Vivaldi and Pachabel may help settle restless kids. Other composers such as Debussy, Copland, Lee, Halpern-Kelly or Stivland are also used for relaxation. If your child prefers, you can resort to soothing nature sounds or gentle ambient tunes.

10. Worry Unloading Activities

Choose one or more of the following:

- **Beat the WorryBug** - See Activity One.

- **Give it a Rest** - Use the following activity before bedtime. Let the kids draw or write what's worrying them and put their problem in the night table drawer. It will be something to think about the next day. You can use Wince as their guardian soft toy or you can assign this job to one of a number of small dolls. If you use the latter, place each doll on the night stand or foot of the bed and give it one specific responsibility. It may be something like keeping mom or dad safe from danger or whatever the child is worried about.

- **The Worry Tree** - Place some type of tree or a Happy Plant near the front door. As the child comes in from their hassled world, they can leave their problem behind by simply touching a leaf and saying their worry. The message is to leave their worry outside. This measure allows kids to unload their burden before settling in at home, so they can feel care-free in their home environment.

- **Worry Exhauster** - Use a bit of surprising reverse psychology on uptight kids needing a tension reliever. Have the child physically exhaust his/her energy through some exercise outlet. A trampoline, a swing, or a running or climbing activity would be great, as would any safely supervised sport. Just get them to move, move, move!

- **Worry Time** - Have a little ritual for a certain time each day. At this given hour, the kids are invited to share their worries on how to beat the WorryBug. These ideas can be written down and discussed. This strategy means you address their concerns at that time. It will stop them from coming to you all day with their issues. That way, each time the worrying issue is raised, you can say "That worry sounds like it's important to talk about because it's giving you a hard time. Let's write it down and later we can really talk about it properly. Till then, let's try not to let it bug us."

11. Massage (for children under 8)

You may have noticed that the kids who are the least relaxed or more likely to "explode" in anger are often poor cuddlers. Their "emotional electricity" has not been soothed. Children need grounding energy or cuddling to soothe and settle their emotions. Nearly every child likes to be massaged at some point on their bodies—such as the forearm, neck or back, or even a good rub on the scalp. Try and find that special spot. Also choose a time—after their shower or bath is often good—when they would enjoy this activity.

Car Wash Method

Have the child lie on his/her back with their eyes closed. Gently hold each arm and pretend they're going through a car wash,

- Rinse cycle - Gently run your fingers from their shoulders to their fingers
- Wash cycle - Gently massage the arm like the soft car wash brushes
- The Rag wash - Tickle his/her arm with a soft rag or cloth
- Final Rinse - Run your fingers up and down each arm
- Blow Dry - Blow gently on each arm

Weather Report Method

This is one activity that is easy to learn, feels good and is one weather report that can accurately forecast a cool change!

Snowflakes
Tap fingers rapidly and lightly on the child's head, shoulders and back.

Raindrops
Same as for snowflakes but a little harder.

Thunderclaps
Cup your hands and clap them across the back and shoulders.

Tornado
Place your hands on the child's shoulders and circle your thumbs down either side of the spine and across the shoulders.

Tidal wave
Slide your hands up and down the arms and across the back.

Calm after the storm
Rest your hands on, then above, his/her shoulders for a few moments. Then step back.

Appendix

These worksheets will help you and your little worried one get on their way to conquering the WorryBug!

ANXIETY CHECKLIST

Review the following chart and then rate your child's anxiety level. You may want to use a number system ranging from 1-10. The most frequent/serious characteristics would be rated higher, whereas rare/mild symptoms would be rated lower.

	Date	Date	Date
Dry mouth and swallowing difficulty or hoarseness			
Rapid breathing and heartbeat			
Twitching or trembling			
Muscle tension and headache			
Appetite changes			
Sweating			
Nausea, diarrhea and weight loss			
Sleeplessness			
Hyperventilation			
Irritability			
Fatigue			
Nightmares			
Frequent urination			
Memory problems			
Constant seeking of attention and reassurance			

Make sure to review What's Bugging My Child (p9) after completing the anxiety checklist.

WORRY WINNING LADDER WORKSHEET - PART 1 DATE:___________

Directions: Make a list of your worries. Then rate each worry from 1 to 10 -big worries are given high scores and little worries given low scores. Place these worries on the rungs of the ladder in ascending order with the least bothersome worry on the bottom rung. Cross out and date each worry when it has been conquered!
(Refer to p26 for full directions.)

WORRY LIST	Rating

WORRY
WINNING
LADDER
WORKSHEET
PART 2
PRIZE
DATE________

WorryBug Notes

We hope that you have enjoyed our booklet and that it has provided you with background and activities to help your little worrier adjust to life in a complex and changing world. If your child has specific anxieties that haven't been covered in this booklet, you may want to check out a copy of one of my DVDs. The collection includes the whole gamut of kids' issues. They are available through my clinic at www.drjohnshappyfamilies.com.au. In addition, The WorryWoo family of books and plush critters also deals with a number of emotions in an amusing and practical way. These cuddly creatures should help put a smile on everyone's face! They can be found at WorryWoos.com. Once again, if you need additional help in coping with your children's psychological issues, please chat with your doctor or a well-respected local clinical psychologist.

Best wishes for a happy and healthy life together.
Good luck beating the WorryBug!

Helping Young Worriers Beat The WorryBug is the foundation booklet for the whole WorryWoo series, if you or your child would like specific help with anxiety related topics then check out the booklets as follow:

Anxiety related issue - Dr. John booklet	Accompanying WorryWoo Books
• Loneliness – friendlessness, rejection	The Lonely Little Monster (Nola)
• Anxious/withdrawn	The Monster In The Bubble (Squeek)
• Self esteem, bullying and body image	The Nose That Didn't Fit (Rue)
• Indecision and low self confidence	The Monster Who Couldn't Decide (Fuddle)
• Frustration and poor self control	The Very Frustrated Monster (Twitch)